Daphne's Dive

BOOKS BY QUIARA ALEGRÍA HUDES PUBLISHED BY TCG

Daphne's Dive

Elliot, A Soldier's Fugue

The Happiest Song Plays Last

Water by the Spoonful

Daphne's Dive

———

Quiara Alegría Hudes

THEATRE COMMUNICATIONS GROUP
NEW YORK
2017

The publication of *Daphne's Dive* by Quiara Alegría Hudes, through TCG's Book Program, is made possible in part by the New York State Council on the Arts with the support of Governor Andrew Cuomo and the New York State Legislature.

TCG books are exclusively distributed to the book trade by Consortium Book Sales and Distribution.

Library of Congress Control Numbers:
2016045501 (print) / 2016053187 (ebook)
ISBN 978-1-55936-531-4 (paperback) / ISBN 978-1-55936-857-5 (ebook)
A catalog record for this book is available from the Library of Congress.

Book design and composition by Lisa Govan
Cover design by Rodrigo Corral and Zak Tebbal

First Edition, October 2017

In memory:
Kathy Chang(e)

———

Daphne's Dive

PRODUCTION HISTORY

Daphne's Dive had its world premiere at Signature Theatre Company (James Houghton, Founding Artistic Director; Erika Mallin, Executive Director) in New York City, on May 15, 2016. It was directed by Thomas Kail. The original music was by Michel Camilo, the scenic design was by Donyale Werle, the lighting design was by Betsy Adams, the costume design was by Toni-Leslie James, the sound design was by Nevin Steinberg; the production stage manager was Lori Ann Zepp. The cast was:

DAPHNE	Vanessa Aspillaga
INEZ	Daphne Rubin-Vega
ACOSTA	Carlos Gomez
REY	Gordon Joseph Weiss
JENN	K.K. Moggie
PABLO	Matt Saldivar
RUBY	Samira Wiley

CHARACTERS

DAPHNE, a bar owner, Latina

INEZ, Daphne's sister, Latina

ACOSTA, Inez's husband, Latino

REY, a glass cutter and manual laborer, any ethnicity

JENN, an activist, performance artist and merrymaker, Asian-American

PABLO, a painter, Latino

RUBY, a young woman who is also in some way a child, any ethnicity

SETTING

Philadelphia, 1994–2011

SCENE 1

North Philly. Piano music tumbles out of a second-story window.

RUBY: I am eleven.

(Into: Daphne's Dive—a corner bar in North Philadelphia. A potted aloe vera plant by the window. Pablo drinks orange juice. Rey nurses a beer. They hear the piano music from upstairs.)

PABLO: That's one helluva rooster.

DAPHNE: Those eighty-eight get beat like a birthday piñata.

PABLO: You admire him more than me.

DAPHNE: Live music every morning? I ain't complaining.

PABLO: There's more to art than pretty songs.

DAPHNE: Ay, you're my favorite artist, okay?

PABLO: Okay.

DAPHNE: It's not a contest.

PABLO: Yes it is.

(She splashes some vodka in his orange juice.)

DAPHNE: For inspiration.

PABLO: Isn't Acosta usually through by now?

REY: You waiting on Acosta? Me, too.

(Daphne pours a Coke from the tap.)

PABLO: What's with all the Coca-Cola? It's barely eleven.

DAPHNE: Yeah, my stomach is protesting, but those sirens, all night? You didn't hear from the corner?

PABLO: Nah, I was sketching and blasting Vivaldi.

DAPHNE: My upstairs tenants, above the piano player? Three nights ago, cops raid the place. Two nights ago, *feds* raid the place. Last night, one in the morning: Wham! Whack! "F you, B! Suck this!" Playing baseball with the furniture.

PABLO: That's what you get, not evicting them years ago.

DAPHNE: All those kids running, screaming, *carajo*, they have more kids than the old lady who lived in a shoe. Feds took the parents in handcuffs. DHS rounded up the children. The little boy, the one who can't walk, beautiful clear eyes, wearing rags, Pablo. Cuando hay un Salvation Army two blocks away. In the United States of America, you gonna dress your kids like a shantytown? So I'm tired. I'm tired and I'll be drinking Coca-Cola all day.

PABLO: At least one of 'em got out. The older boy. Navy, was it?

DAPHNE: Last week he comes home. His "tour of duty" is up. We're chatting in the stairwell. Kid never stepped foot in boot camp. "Navy," it turns out, means Graterford Prison.

PABLO: Maximum security!

DAPHNE: Just eighteen years old, so you know he did some heavy shit. I gave him a mop and a ten and he cleaned the hell outta my stairwell.

PABLO: Ten bucks won't keep him off the street.

DAPHNE: It'll keep him outta my face.

PABLO: You need a proper coffee.

DAPHNE: I can't. My reflux.

PABLO: So brew it light.

DAPHNE: My Krups broke.

PABLO: I'll go to Lawrence Bakery. How do you take it?

DAPHNE: Why you being so nice?

PABLO: I have a favor.

DAPHNE: Not my trash.

PABLO: Daphne.

DAPHNE: You know I don't go for that.

PABLO: I started a new canvas.

DAPHNE: My garbage, my business.

PABLO: You take sugar?

DAPHNE: Two equals, skim milk. The answer's still no.

(Pablo exits. Daphne has a stomach pang. Using a knife, she removes a chunk from the potted aloe and dissects it for the gel inside.)

That your motorcycle out front?

REY: Goldwing GL.

DAPHNE: What club you ride with?

REY: Whole point is to get away from folks.

DAPHNE: The guy I was just talking to, he paints bikes. He came through one time with a Harley-Davidson, whole thing airbrushed with eagles, buffalos, tomahawks—a powwow on wheels. Following week he showed up with a trophy tall as this bar.

REY: You ever ride?

DAPHNE: There's two kinds of people. Those who ride bikes and those who don't wanna die. Roy is it?

REY: Rey.

DAPHNE: Welcome back.

(Daphne has removed the gelatinous "meat" from the aloe. She slurps it down whole, like a live fish, and grimaces.)

Ach ayy blaghghg!

REY: Too much drink?

DAPHNE: Too much life.

(Jenn enters. Her sequined American flag bikini shows off a lithe figure. Over each breast is a blue glittery star; the bikini bottom is red-and-white stripes. The effect is not sexual but striking and bold. Her handmade flag reads: PEACE LIBERTY ECOLOGY DEMOCRACY. It's ripped down the middle.)

JENN: Beautiful day for a dance in the sun.

DAPHNE: Art Museum Steps?

JENN: Best real estate in the city, and it's mine.

DAPHNE: What did the cops have to say?

JENN: They might as well have had 3-D glasses and tubs of popcorn. They were cracking up. Called me every name in the book. But there were a lot of school groups today.

Wide-eyed children, so curious, completely open, and they can't look away. "Hey miss, why you dance like that?" "Hey miss, let me wave that flag!" I had a whole class of first graders chanting, "Peace! Liberty! Ecology! Democracy!" The cops pulled out handcuffs, Daphne.

DAPHNE: To arrest you or the kids?

JENN: They chased me around the Calder sculpture, through all the soft pretzel stands. One of 'em ripped my flag and the first graders booed him.

DAPHNE: Coffee and rum?

JENN: Please.

DAPHNE: Oh shit, my Krups broke.

JENN: Just rum then. How's it going?

REY: What's the occasion?

JENN: Another day on planet Earth.

REY: You always dress like that?

DAPHNE: In the winter she wears more fabric.

JENN: Liberty Bell on Sundays. Love Statue during the week. UPenn, Art Museum Steps. It's *my* Contract with America. Not that Newt Gingrich approves . . .

REY: Who's Newt Gingrich?

JENN: Bless your soul. *(To Daphne)* Has Acosta come through yet?

DAPHNE: Take a number.

(Jenn mends her flag. Inez, Daphne's older sister, enters. It's clear she shops at fancier stores than Daphne.)

INEZ: Coño, that traffic would make Mahatma Gandhi an asshole. *(To Jenn)* I love it.

DAPHNE: Hey sis! How's the Main Line?

INEZ: No tienes ninguna idea, Daphne. These gringos . . .

DAPHNE: Suburbanite, you miss us. Hehehe . . .

INEZ: No. You think I miss breathing the pollution from all these SEPTA buses? I'm just acclimating to the provincial mentality of my new neighbors.

DAPHNE: The people next door again?

INEZ: I put up an eight-foot picket fence so I didn't have to see their ratty underwear. Hired the best carpenter on the Main Line, custom-made, beautiful pine. I didn't move to Haverford to see some tighty-whities on a clothesline out my kitchen window. They're environmentalists, but really? Did we have a washer and drier in Puerto Rico?

DAPHNE: You know we didn't.

INEZ: No we did not but you'd never see Mami's bra blowing in the breeze, waving at the neighbors. Am I right?

DAPHNE: Mami didn't wear a bra a day in her life.

INEZ: Well her underwear. Papi's underwear. Am I right?

DAPHNE: Always and forever, sis.

INEZ: And they were pissed I put up the fence. Bringing me a fresh-baked pie, explaining that picket fences aren't "what we do here." "The trees belong to all of us." What was I going to do, tell her, "Hey, Mother Earth, I don't want to see the brown stripes up and down your husband's draws?"

DAPHNE: Delicious, thank you.

INEZ: They know and I know what's under it all: "Porta Rickins" bought the best house in the zip code. Sorry, Charlie! Eat it up, Haverford! So, I planted a güiro vine at the base of the picket fence, because I'm connected to my roots. No Boricua garden should exist without a güiro vine. Coño, you should see my güiros.

JENN: What's a güiro?

INEZ: A güiro is a gourd, a calabash. More Puerto Rican than a crucifix on the rearview. Más Boricua que un parakeet in the kitchen.

DAPHNE: Scratchy instrument we play around the holidays.

INEZ: You should see my güiros, they're bulging like Schwarzenegger muscles. Son como *Little Shop of Horrors*. No joda, Daphne, if you saw my güiros, you'd have a heart attack.

DAPHNE: Jesus Christ, then bring me a fucking güiro already.

INEZ: I knew you'd want one!

(Inez pulls a large gourd from her pocketbook, hands it to Daphne.)

So the vine grows tall, and one güiro flops over the picket fence to the other side. Onto the neighbor's side. And what do they do? Do they push it back to my side? They took their garden shears and chopped off the güiro.

DAPHNE: Inez, you can buy a güiro for a dollar twenty-nine at any local market.

INEZ: That's not the point.

DAPHNE: What's the point?!

INEZ: That nobody better touch my güiro!

(Daphne pokes it.)

DAPHNE: I touched your güiro.

(Rey does, too.)

REY: That makes two of us.

(Jenn tickles it.)

JENN: Hey little calabash.

INEZ: Ya'll can kiss my behind.

DAPHNE: Rum punch?

INEZ: Ginger ale.

DAPHNE: How am I supposed to keep my lights on, people? This is a bar, not a soda fountain.

INEZ: You need some extra money? Sell my güiros.

DAPHNE: Oh my god.

(Pablo enters, puts a small coffee on the bar, and another beside it.)

PABLO: Tu cafecito and a backup, in case of emergency.

(Inez reaches for the extra coffee. Pablo whacks her hand playfully.)

For Daphne only.

INEZ: She's got an ulcer like the ozone hole. *(Hands Daphne the newspaper)* Mira, your tenants are in the paper. Change the locks. You want Acosta to do it?

DAPHNE: As soon as possible, thanks. *(Reading)* Jesus, they found guns up there?

INEZ: Now DHS is going to split up all those siblings.

(Acosta appears, regal and confident. He dresses well, even on the site of his construction jobs. He carries an enormous beat-up cardboard box.)

ACOSTA: Someone grab the door!

DAPHNE: There he is.

(He drops the box at Jenn's feet. She digs in: bandannas.)

JENN: They're rainbow colored!

ACOSTA: How'd I guess?

INEZ: Hi, Papi.

ACOSTA: What's up, Mami?

INEZ: I'm starving. Want to go to Indian Palace?

ACOSTA: I got some loose ends to tie up. Gimme an hour.

INEZ: So . . . ? Don't tell me the city threw another hurdle in your path.

ACOSTA: Nope. I got the contract.

INEZ: Chulisimo. A mini mall on Allegheny, time to celebrate!

ACOSTA: In an hour.

INEZ: I need a hundred dollars.

ACOSTA: What happened to the three hundred I gave you this morning?

INEZ: Daphne needs new locks.

ACOSTA *(Handing Inez money)*: I'll have one of my guys put them in later. Oh, negra, I spoke with the lawyer. He said it same as me. Ain't nobody gonna touch my gatdamned güiros.

INEZ: We will sue their asses.

DAPHNE: Judge Wapner, here comes crazy güiro lady!

INEZ: Sheeee-it.

(Inez kisses Acosta, exits. Acosta approaches Rey.)

ACOSTA: Rey!

REY: Acosta!

ACOSTA: Long time no see! Where you been?

REY: St. Louis, Atlanta, here and there. *(Showing a photo)* Check out my grandson. I rode down to West Virginia, gave him his first baseball. So you're in the glass business now.

ACOSTA: Changing the face of the neighborhood. North Philly used to be brick walls, block after block, far as you could see, right? Tiny windows. Row homes that looked like prisons.

REY: Who laid them bricks with you?

ACOSTA: Now, go up Allegheny, go up Fifth and Lehigh, check out my storefronts, office buildings, my residential facades: floor-to-ceiling windows. An entire community and I'm letting in the light.

REY: You name it, I can do it. Windowpanes, etching, shower stalls.

ACOSTA *(Impressed)*: Etching?

REY: The boss had me dedicate a Chanel bottle to his wife.

ACOSTA: A hundred and twenty a day. Flat fee, if it's four hours or eighteen.

REY: Cash?

ACOSTA: Payroll, everything on the books now.

REY: Acosta gone legit. I'm still cash only.

ACOSTA: You're too old for that!

REY: Can you pay me daily? Too big a wallet, I get in trouble.

ACOSTA: A hundred and twenty cash, in your hand, before you leave the warehouse every day?

REY: Can I start at noon?

ACOSTA: You should be my negotiator!

REY: I'm not a morning person.

ACOSTA: Daphne, Rey used to run my crew back when I did all the brickwork from Girard to Lehigh, when everything was under the table. End of day I'd put cash in his hand, he'd get on his bike, eat, drink, gamble till his pockets were empty. Show up the next day, do it all over again. And you know what? He's happy. You still happy?

REY: Never die with money in your pocket.

ACOSTA *(To Rey)*: Allegheny and Mascher, the blue warehouse, tomorrow at noon.

(They shake. Rey unfolds a map, studies it. Sensing his moment, Pablo approaches.)

PABLO: Acosta, oye, I was up by Mascher. What do I see? Warehouse, open lot, warehouse. No one can tell there's business being conducted there. Now picture this: hand-painted letters. Acosta Glass Company.

ACOSTA: Corporation.

PABLO: Acosta Glass Corporation. Visibility, a little style.

ACOSTA: We work behind the scenes. It's not a storefront. No one needs to know we're there.

PABLO: A sign is a presence.

ACOSTA: You short on rent?

PABLO: My landlord's cool.

ACOSTA: I'm not that cool.

PABLO: I'm short on paint. There's two eight-by-eight canvases taped to my living room wall. I've sketched it all out. Mapped it by pencil. Garbage from Edison.

DAPHNE: Edison High? You went through their trash?

PABLO: Five A.M., three days straight.

DAPHNE: Physically inside those dumpsters?

PABLO: Knee-deep in pencil shavings, milk cartons. You know what else is in those dumpsters? These kids, our community's future? Their work. It's a high school but the handwriting, you think kindergartners wrote some of it. I fill my shopping cart, wheel it home, arrange all this trash on my living room floor, then I sketch the composition onto the canvas. Pencil only, cuz without paint . . . Mine is a very expensive hobby. I should've been a poet.

ACOSTA: No one wants a painting of trash.

PABLO: Shit.

ACOSTA: Your work is awesome but who wants it hanging above their sofa?

PABLO: There's decay in the world. Broken pipes, shattered windows. You fix them, I record them.

ACOSTA: The day you're ready to be partners.

QUIARA ALEGRÍA HUDES

PABLO: No!

ACOSTA: Hear me out.

PABLO: I'm no businessman.

ACOSTA: The yellow lines down every Philly street? The same family has had that contract for a hundred years. You know what that contract is worth?

PABLO: Headaches?

ACOSTA: Dollars. Millions. The city put out a call for proposals. We write a business plan, split all profits down the middle.

PABLO: Six years I was in Stockholm, collecting garbage. Pick up the bin, toss it in the hopper, day after shitty day. Now let me paint you one sign so I can go afford one tube of cerulean goddamn blue!

ACOSTA: See? That's the problem with this neighborhood. You can't teach a man to fish anymore. By the time I was fifteen I was running both my dad's groceries.

PABLO: Fifteen? Who remembers fifteen? At that age I was in Cuba eating mangos for breakfast. You see this gray hair?

ACOSTA: No.

PABLO: Death's practically at my door. I can't be owing another man shit.

ACOSTA: Owing? Fifty-fifty split!

PABLO: You have poor taste in art.

ACOSTA: Forget it.

PABLO: Go buy some palm tree paintings from the cultural center.

ACOSTA: Paint a palm tree, and I'll buy it!

PABLO: I'll be late on rent. Daphne, can I look through your trash?

DAPHNE: No.

PABLO: Let me look through your goddamn trash!

DAPHNE: No.

PABLO: My Edison painting needs a counterpart. What

happens to the children who make this trash? They grow up, they make a different kind of trash. They go to the bar, they come to your doorstep, Daphne, and leave a trail of empties. Milk cartons to beer bottles. Two side-by-side canvases.

DAPHNE: Pablo, por favor, if I give you a Heineken will you shut the fuck up about my trash?

PABLO: I suppose. Yes. Thank you.

(She gives him a beer. He sips it, sadly. A momentary lull as everyone feels bad for Pablo. Rey approaches.)

REY: Is a tube of paint expensive?

PABLO: Depends on the size.

REY *(Handing him money)*: Will this get you some supplies?

PABLO: And a few sips of inspiration. *(Signaling to Daphne)* Put it towards my tab.

REY: That blue Goldwing out front, I'd like to get her painted.

PABLO: The whole chassis?

REY: Covered in mermaids.

PABLO: Rated PG?

REY: PG-13.

PABLO: My customs have brought in fifteen thousand.

REY: And you can't afford a tube of paint?

PABLO: Eh.

REY: Maybe I can hire you bit by bit.

PABLO: This will get you one small mermaid.

REY: All right.

PABLO: Waist up.

REY: Then how can you tell she's a mermaid?

PABLO: The seashells.

REY: I'll leave her here tomorrow at noon. *(Extending his hand)* Rey.

PABLO: Pablo. *(They shake)*
ACOSTA: Congratulations, Picasso! Don't look so depressed.
PABLO: Son-of-a-bitch, this is me looking happy. Time to celebrate. Time to dig through Daphne's trash.
DAPHNE: Oh no you don't.
PABLO: Hit me, punch me, kick me. I'm going see the shit we all throw away.

(He exits through the back door.)

JENN: Thanks for the blindfolds.
ACOSTA *(To Daphne)*: She cleaned my house, she wouldn't take cash. I paid her with four hundred bandannas.
DAPHNE: What were you doing with four hundred bandannas in the first place?
ACOSTA: I know a guy.
JENN: Last year was my dance-in. My sing-in before that. This year is going to be my see-in. A huge crowd at City Hall, we'll take off the blindfolds in unison. You coming, Daphne?

(Daphne's not coming.)

How about you, Acosta?
ACOSTA: God gave me two eyes for a reason.
JENN: To bear witness. Your own foreman got arrested, got pulverized, for what? Looking a cop in the eye? Our tax dollars paid for that.
ACOSTA: You pay taxes?
JENN: Sales tax.
ACOSTA: You barter everything. I bring jobs into the community, that's my protest.

JENN: Don't act like we never got arrested together. For blocking rush-hour traffic on Market Street. *(Beat)* Hey, the city padlocked my squat.

ACOSTA: I'll have Inez show you a few apartments.

JENN: I can't pay rent.

ACOSTA: The only rentals I have are the kind where you pay rent.

JENN: Give me an unused warehouse, I'll clean it out free. Just till I get back on my feet.

DAPHNE: She scrubs my floor like a badass. I could eat off that linoleum.

ACOSTA: I've got an empty place on Dauphin. It's a real mess. Three months, not a day over.

(Jenn puts the finishing touches on her flag.)

JENN: Mind if I?

DAPHNE: Give it a spin, please.

(Jenn's dance moves are original, graceful, and yet unsettling. Her legs and arms swirl as the flag waves. Her performance swells in intensity and beauty—this woman can really dance, even if her style is strange.)

PABLO: Daphne.

(Pablo has entered from the back. Propped in his arms is a girl, covered in tiny cuts. Jenn stops dancing.)

DAPHNE: Oh my god, what . . . ? She was out back?

PABLO: Behind the dumpster. The third-floor window is shattered.

DAPHNE: She must have jumped when the cops rounded up her family. *(To Acosta)* Pull your truck around. *(To Jenn)* Cover her. *(To Pablo)* Water.

(Acosta exits. Jenn wraps Ruby in her flag.)

Baby girl, it's Daphne, from downstairs. Mira, glass *in* her skin. Jesus.

(Pablo brings water.)

Baby girl . . . take a drink? One sip.

(Ruby manages a sip.)

There you go. Were you out there all night?

RUBY: My little brother, he don't walk right, his joints click at the hip. Cops was banging at the door, my mom said, "Run, hide yourselves." I left my brother. And then I was falling.

SCENE 2

From the upstairs window, piano music.

RUBY: I am fifteen.

(Into: Daphne's Dive, four years later, evening. Changes mark the passing of time: most notably, a girl's sneaker is affixed to the bar. The potted aloe's still there. Campaign posters declare: ACOSTA FOR COUNCILMAN-AT-LARGE. Daphne sets out snacks, catering trays, drinks. Pablo, Jenn and Ruby paint finishing touches onto a banner. The TV news is on mute and they all glance at it frequently.)

REY: My gramps rode the rails in the Great Depression. He didn't need more than a sandwich in his bucket and he'd make do. If Acosta loses tonight I'm taking you on a ride.

DAPHNE: After all you've had to drink?

REY: Hey Ruby, has your mom ever left this bar?

RUBY: I've never seen her from the waist down.

REY: There's a new bridge on the Susquehanna, we'll glide over it like birds.

DAPHNE: I'm a mammal, honey. A mammal who is throwing a party.

REY: Not if Acosta loses.

DAPHNE: Celebration, consolation, I'm throwing a party.

REY: Well, this weekend? The Susquehanna ain't going nowhere.

DAPHNE: And leave Ruby alone?

REY: She's fifteen.

DAPHNE: I gotta work.

REY: When the bar closes.

DAPHNE: And sleep where?

REY: Nowhere, just ride there and back.

DAPHNE: What's the point of riding a motorcycle in the dark?

REY: Crossing the Monongahela at night? You can't see a thing but you hear the water below. You lose your stomach and sprout wings.

DAPHNE: You think I'm gonna wrap my legs around some asymmetrical mermaid titties?

PABLO: Hey. They are not asymmetrical.

DAPHNE: And if it rains?

REY: Then we ride in the rain.

DAPHNE: And if it pours?

RUBY: Rey, stop flirting and come give us a hand?

(They hang the hand-painted banner: CITY COUNCILMAN JOE ACOSTA. Inez and Acosta enter, all nervous energy.)

INEZ: Take that down, it's bad luck!

ACOSTA: They have to prepare for the party, negra.

INEZ: What party? Knock wood, take it down! Rub the lucky shoe!

(They take down the banner as Inez rubs the shoe on the bar.)

ACOSTA: They're calling the whole thing in the next ten minutes.

PABLO: Shouldn't you be at your headquarters?

ACOSTA: Too much pressure. And if I win, I can make a big entrance.

RUBY: Nervous?

ACOSTA: Yup.

INEZ: He just drank a bottle of Mylanta.

RUBY: Want to hear my speech?

ACOSTA: You'll do fine.

DAPHNE: Let her practice.

ACOSTA: Trust me, I won't hear a word right now.

(Inez holds up a padded envelope.)

INEZ: Well, Papi, God is good. This is your ticket, viejo. Surprise.

ACOSTA: From Antonio Acosta, P.R.?

(Acosta opens it, pulls out an old suit. Aged at the seams, fabric and cut from a different era, but meticulously cared for. There is a letter enclosed.)

"Dear Joe, Six generations of Acosta men have worn this. It's crossed islands, continents, oceans. Now it's in your hands. Treat it right. Mend any holes, starch it and when the time comes, send it to the next Acosta man who needs it." *(Amazed)* It's the suit.

INEZ: Does your old lady got your back, or what?

ACOSTA: My pop used to tell these stories. That for generations every Acosta man shared one suit. Mailed it back and forth, in an envelope. Because we were poor, but it became tradition. I thought, "Okay, whatever you say, Pop, never let the truth ruin a good story, right?" But it exists . . . Negra, how on earth . . .

INEZ: Put it on, the clock is ticking.

(He goes to the bathroom but the door is locked.)

DAPHNE: The toilet flooded.

INEZ: Change out here, apúrate!

ACOSTA: Everyone look away.

INEZ: You might be blinded by the sight of Acosta's chicken legs.

(Acosta changes.)

You want to know about a wild-goose chase? The number of Acostas I had to call? I was pulling Acostas out of the woodwork. Area codes, country codes, corners of the earth . . . And I made some fast enemies, too. Women like, "Puñeta, don't you ever call my man again!"

(Reading the letter:)

JENN: Check it out. A list of everyone who's worn the suit.

RUBY: "Miguel Gallard Acosta, wedding, Puerto Rico. Hernan Acosta, baptism, Chicago. Fransisco Suarez, funeral, Orlando. Charles Acosta, one-hundredth birthday, Brooklyn."

JENN: "Bronx Legal Aid Society, first trial."

RUBY: "Mayoral inauguration, Loíza."
JENN: "Family portrait, Hawaii . . ."

(Acosta models the jacket.)

PABLO: Ay bendito, that's adorable!
ACOSTA: I can't wear this thing.
PABLO: A suit for a teeny-tiny Acosta.
INEZ: Guapo, it's a true power suit. Jenn, can you take out the sleeves?

(Jenn inspects the cuffs.)

JENN: There's enough fabric. I got my kit.
INEZ: They're watching out for you, Papi, all the Acosta men. Maferefún!

(Jenn begins to alter the suit, sewing deftly, hemming with agility.)

REY: Ticker says you're sixty-two percent in the Northeast.
INEZ: Go 'head! All them gringos voting for quality!
PABLO: Quality my ass.
ACOSTA: Up yours.
REY: The Northeast is blue collar. They like a working man.
INEZ: They respect a born-and-bred Catholic with the balls to criticize Cardinal Bevilacqua. My husband ain't gonna bow to no man who condemns the use of a rubber. Who says I'm going to hell for using a diaphragm? Think about it.
PABLO: No thank you.
RUBY: What's a diaphragm?
DAPHNE: Something she stopped needing a long time ago.

INEZ: Birth control for married women. You just worry about condoms—they protect against pregnancy *and* STDs.

DAPHNE: Change the subject.

REY: Thank you.

INEZ: Prude.

DAPHNE: She's fifteen.

INEZ: Exactly, fifteen is the new forty. This is the stuff Mami was never frank about. *(To Ruby)* Next week I'll bring a banana and a condom.

DAPHNE: Drop it, Inez.

INEZ: Unlike you, we can't all be the Virgin Mary on our wedding night.

(Daphne shatters a glass in the sink.)

DAPHNE: What?

INEZ: Shit.

RUBY: You were married?

ACOSTA: Do you two have to get into it at this moment?

DAPHNE: You. Outside.

(Inez follows Daphne out to the curb.)

INEZ: Learn to laugh at yourself. *(Silence)* It was my nerves, Daph.

DAPHNE: Ruby's not a virgin.

INEZ: Then she needs information on how to stay protected.

DAPHNE: Her stepfather, Inez. Why do you think DHS let me adopt her? Even with the mom fighting tooth and nail?

INEZ: Who else have you told?

DAPHNE: The police, DHS, the adoption agency.

INEZ: How old was Ruby? Was it one time? Many times?

DAPHNE: Unlike you, I respect people's privacy.

INEZ: Put her in therapy.

DAPHNE: I do. I eat ramen to pay for her sessions.

INEZ: But you never asked my advice?

DAPHNE: How is this about you?

INEZ: Do you need money?

DAPHNE: So you can lord it over my head?

INEZ: There's a surgery to reconstruct the hymen.

DAPHNE: Are you out of your fucking mind?

INEZ: She needs to be normalized. I didn't found Women's Way for nothing. I talk to girls like her every day. Girls worse off.

DAPHNE: Yeah, you save every stranger who calls that hotline.

INEZ: Allow Ruby the grace of getting it out in the open. No secrecy.

DAPHNE: Coming from you, that's a masterpiece. *(Silence)*

INEZ: That was different. We were children.

DAPHNE: You were a teenager. And Mami asked you to keep your mouth shut and you did.

INEZ: Because I was naive. You think if I understood the full extent of things . . . ?

DAPHNE: You knew enough to avoid Papi like the plague. And to avoid looking me in the eye for years.

INEZ: You were my baby doll. Still are.

DAPHNE: You are not to talk to my daughter about sex.

INEZ: Ruby is a virgin. Teach her that. Look her in the eye every night and say, "Ruby, tu eres una virgen."

(Ruby comes outside.)

RUBY: Are you two talking about me?

INEZ: Give us another minute, kiddo?

DAPHNE: Stay out here. Any news?

RUBY: He lost Germantown.

(Inez goes into the bar.)

You were married?

DAPHNE: Come on, I want to hear your speech.

RUBY: You were married, Mom?

DAPHNE: The ceremony outlasted the marriage. A Catholic mass so long, time started to reverse on itself.

RUBY: What was his name?

DAPHNE: Tomorrow I'll pull out the box and show you a few photos, okay?

RUBY: You said you've never been in love. I thought, maybe she's not attracted to men . . .

DAPHNE: Not the ones who come through here.

RUBY: Women, then?

DAPHNE: Boy girl black brown yellow polka dot, people are knuckleheads.

RUBY: If you ever want to go on a date, I can tuck myself in at night.

DAPHNE: I own a bar. I need two feet to stand, two hands to mix, a brain to add. All these other parts? Extraneous.

RUBY: Have you ever had a wet dream?

DAPHNE: That's a boy thing.

RUBY: I read a book that said girls get them, too.

DAPHNE: What book?

RUBY: It said girls can have them.

DAPHNE: Have you had one?

(Silence.)

Is there someone at school you can ask?

RUBY: I go to Holy Innocents. Sex Ed is like: "Touch your privates, burn in hell."

DAPHNE: Okay. I gotta go prep.

RUBY: So am I gonna burn in hell?

DAPHNE: If you've done that, I'm sure it's fine, you don't need my permission.

RUBY: Have you ever, like one time?

DAPHNE: Maybe when I was a kid, I don't remember.

(Silence.)

No, Ruby. I've never done that.

(Jenn appears.)

JENN: Fits him like a glove. Suit looks damn fine.

RUBY: Go. Prep.

(Daphne exits into the bar.)

JENN: You nervous, Ruby Slippers?

RUBY: About a speech? After all the times you've had me dancing at the Love Statue?

JENN: My dad used to get cheap suits, make me hem the pants, pin the jackets. Polyester so thick, the needles would break in half. But I learned to sew. He always said, *(Chinese accent)* "My daughter is sinful American, my wife is terrible Christian. My only companion is suit on my back." The day he kicked me out, I rammed all his ties down the toilet.

RUBY: Oh shit.

JENN: Jammed 'em in there with the plunger. Then, peed on it.

RUBY: Ew.

JENN: If you get nervous during your speech, think of that.

RUBY: You ever miss them?

JENN: You ever miss yours? *(No response)* I'm the one who found my mom. Came home after school, snuck into her room to grab a few bucks. There she was, face down on the floor. Her grandfather's antique pistol in her hand.

RUBY: You're the only one who doesn't tiptoe around me.

JENN *(A beat)*: I do miss her. Just like the devil misses heaven.

RUBY: Can we go dancing tomorrow?

JENN: What flag I should bring?

RUBY: "What do we want? Complete social transformation! When do we want it? Every day!"

JENN AND RUBY: Every day! Every day!

(Pablo appears at the door.)

PABLO: It's getting down to the wire.

(They head back inside.)

ACOSTA: Just Mantua and Kensington left, final results any minute.

REY: You got nerves of steel, man.

(Pablo raises a drink.)

PABLO: Before you become a big shot and stop answering my calls . . . To Acosta. Whose application of cologne may lack subtlety. Who wears a two-finger ring.

INEZ: That's my viejo.

PABLO: But if there's any artist I look up to . . . Different mediums, different aesthetics. But you made an entire neighborhood your canvas. So if you win this thing, I'm going to give you my largest trash painting to hang above your sofa, you son-of-a-bitch!

ACOSTA: I'll take that!

(They drink.)

RUBY: Can I practice my speech now?

ACOSTA: Go for it.

RUBY *(Handing Jenn the written speech)*: Follow along in case I forget?

ACOSTA: Have Pablo do it since Jenn won't be there.

JENN: I won't?

ACOSTA: Dressed like that?

RUBY: She's been sewing you banners all week.

ACOSTA: That has nothing to do with the press conference.

RUBY: No freaks allowed?

DAPHNE: Don't say freak.

JENN: I prefer witch, libertine, or harpy but freak's good.

ACOSTA: She's dressed for the party, she'll be at the party.

RUBY: I'm not going if she doesn't.

ACOSTA: You're too sensitive.

DAPHNE: Jenn promised she'd stay and help me set up.

JENN: No I didn't.

(Daphne takes the speech and puts it in Pablo's hand.)

DAPHNE: Pablo's got your back, right?

PABLO: Are we friends or are we friends?

RUBY: We're friends.

ACOSTA: Practice the speech.

RUBY *(Can't let it go)*: What are you, embarrassed by her?

ACOSTA: Daphne, get control of this girl. I'm nervous as shit right now!

RUBY: Are you embarrassed by Jenn?

ACOSTA: Not on Halloween.

RUBY: I knew it!

JENN: Next Halloween, go as a shadow of your former self. Go as invasion of the body snatchers.

ACOSTA: Meaning what, exactly?

DAPHNE: Deep breath.

JENN: Turncoat.

INEZ: Hey!

ACOSTA: Beggar!

JENN: Anyone remember Acosta who fed the homeless? Who cuffed himself to the precinct steps? Who marched at my side? No one. Breathe easy, I won't touch your press conference. DuPont? Aria Health? They commit crimes against humanity and you're licking caviar off their toast points.

RUBY: Stop it, both of you.

ACOSTA: Me?!

JENN: For the record, I didn't vote today.

(Silence.)

REY: I didn't vote either. I was hungover.

ACOSTA *(To Rey)*: Thank you. *(To Jenn)* Next time you need a favor, don't come to me. *(To Ruby)* Now the speech.

INEZ: Imagine a hundred cameras in your face.

RUBY *(Rattled)*: Congratulations City Councilman Joe Acosta—

INEZ: Don't say that! Rub the lucky shoe!

RUBY: Congratulations you know who—

INEZ: Lean into the mike so they can hear you.

DAPHNE: Déjala hablar—

ACOSTA: Ya negra.

INEZ: On the podium, there will be a microphone—

PABLO: Just go, Ruby.

RUBY: SHUT UP EVERYONE SHUT UP SHUT UP SHUT UP SHUT UP SHUT UP!

(Ruby cries a bit. Rey offers a bandanna from his pocket.)

REY: It's clean.

RUBY: Congratulations City Councilman Joe Acosta, and congratulations to the voters of Philly. Acosta's my adoptive uncle, but he's more than a dude to watch the Sixers with. Last year he said, "Dream up a project, Ruby, think big, no boundaries, write a business plan, and I'll help you fundraise." Imagine A Nation was born. We visit after-school programs. The kids have to create a flag for a more perfect union. After a sewing lesson with a local artist *(Eyeing Jenn)* they get a needle and thread and become little Betsy Rosses. In our first year alone, two hundred flags, two hundred nations, have been dreamed up, stitch by stitch—

(Acosta's phone rings.)

ACOSTA *(Into the phone)*: Alejandro? *(Listens, hangs up)* I got it.

(Everyone erupts into cheers. "That's it! That's right! Felicidades!" Hugs and applause all around.)

INEZ: Thank you Lord from above!

ACOSTA: You ready?

RUBY: Is the speech okay?

ACOSTA: There won't be a dry eye in the house.

INEZ: Let's show 'em what you got!

DAPHNE *(To Ruby)*: How did God let you fall into my lap? You have fun, okay? *(To Pablo)* Stay with her.

RUBY *(To Jenn)*: You should've voted for him.

JENN: Knock 'em dead, Ruby Slippers.

(Inez, Pablo, Rey, Acosta and Ruby exit. Jenn and Daphne are left alone.)

DAPHNE: Guess we can hang that banner now.

JENN: He doesn't want me in the room? I bless the room from afar.

DAPHNE: Damn sister. Everything she touches turns to gold. Careers, men, bitch hits the numbers more than I do. Fuck 'em?

JENN: Fuck 'em.

(They do a shot.)

I should've voted. My messiah complex got the best of me.

DAPHNE: You don't have a messiah complex, you're just an artist.

JENN: It's my actual diagnosis. Being The Savior is a natural high.

DAPHNE: You think you're God's gift to the world?

JENN: God's alarm clock.

DAPHNE: Shit, if you're the messiah, this round's on me.

DAPHNE AND JENN *(Toasting)*: Fuck 'em!

DAPHNE: Were you the messiah when we first met?

JENN: I was embarrassed about it then. I hadn't developed a sense of humor, which is essential.

DAPHNE: So were you born the messiah?

JENN: Became. After I ditched my husband in San Francisco.

DAPHNE: You got secrets, girl!

JENN: To our husbands?

DAPHNE AND JENN *(Toasting)*: FUCK 'EM!

DAPHNE: I don't even want to know what you wore on your wedding day.

JENN: A veil with eleven colors and a huge papier-mâché mask. When it was time for the vows I took it all off and showed my natural self.

DAPHNE: That's some Ringling Brothers shit.

JENN: He was the Kerouac of Asian America. Poet girls would throw their panties at him. Before the wedding he was bohemian, but after? "Iron my blazer, arrange a car, write a press release." I left for New York, dabbled in that eldest of professions.

DAPHNE: You were a ho?!

JENN: Gotta keep the lights on. Gotta piss off the ex.

DAPHNE: How many dudes you been with?

JENN: "Dudes?"

DAPHNE: Oh, so you're . . .

JENN: Open. And you're . . .

DAPHNE: Catholic.

JENN: I'm no Wilt Chamberlain, but it was the eighties. And then the big a-ha moment. I'm alone in a motel room. Client has left. Feeling low. The door goes creak so I look over but the physical door of the room hasn't moved. It was my heart, opening like a cabinet, so out of use it creaked when it opened. A beautiful voice said, "Today is transformation day. The only thing at stake is the world. So go and dance, go and dance."

DAPHNE: Keep a secret? We waited till our wedding night. And then we were too scared to go through with it.

JENN: How old were you?

DAPHNE: Twenty-four.

JENN: And when you divorced?

DAPHNE: Twenty-four.

Nestor proposed marriage in the third grade. I accepted in the fourth. He bought me a big silver corsage for junior

prom. He made Liberace seem straight. He thought a tra-
ditional marriage would help. The vows would switch up
his spirit, the ceremony would be an eraser, just wipe
away all that shame. He wept both times we had sex. He
took off to New York, got HIV, the disease took him like
that. *(Snaps)* Teamed up, you and Nestor would've turned
the world upside down. Two bright souls born in dark
times.

JENN: Bureaucratic mix-up. I should've been born in the future.

DAPHNE: No. You should've been out there marching with
MLK.

*(Jenn feels Daphne's breasts above her shirt. Jenn's hands
slip underneath Daphne's shirt—feeling something with
concern at first, then curiosity. Daphne pushes Jenn's
hands away.)*

Thank you.

JENN: What happened to your stomach?

DAPHNE *(Noticing)*: Oh shit, Ruby's on TV!

JENN: Turn it up.

DAPHNE: The speaker's been dead for years.

JENN: She looks great.

DAPHNE: Confident, isn't she?

*(Jenn slips her hand into Daphne's, embracing her, as they
watch the TV.)*

There he goes. City Councilman Joe Acosta.

SCENE 3

From the upstairs window, piano music.

RUBY: I am twenty.

> *(Into: The art gallery of a college campus, five years later.
> The walls are hung with paintings of trash.* Ruby wears a
> budget cocktail dress. Pablo, dressed with budget panache,
> holds a small label.)*

PABLO: S-O-L-D. Read it. Say it out loud.
RUBY: Sold.

————

*I imagine we remain in the footprint of the bar. That the "paintings" are
empty frames outlining the bar detritus behind them, framing what we've
seen all along.

PABLO: Great word. Beautiful word. Can I?

RUBY: Put it up? It's your show.

(He places the label beneath a painting.)

PABLO: "Sold." *(Another label)* "Sold."

RUBY: How many labels you got there?

PABLO: Nine.

RUBY: Not bad. Not bad for the opening.

PABLO: You made it to college. And my art made it with you. You are a twenty-year-old abuela. Shuffling around, sprinkling pixie dust, asking nothing in return. *(Sprinkles)* Cariño. *(Sprinkles)* Blao! Cariño.

RUBY: This was completely self-serving. An easy A.

PABLO: My first retrospective, Ruby.

RUBY: Everyone else wrote ten-page papers. I was like, "Can I curate an exhibit?"

PABLO: From Cuba to Stockholm to Philly to Boston University.

RUBY: That old lady bought my piece.

PABLO: "Daphne's Dive?"

RUBY: A thousand broken bottles and you made 'em look like waves on the ocean.

PABLO: Next time I walk into my studio, you know what's gonna greet me? Empty walls. Some of these have been with me so long, when I took them down from the wall, it was a different color behind.

(He pulls a few photographs from an attaché.)

RUBY *(Seeing one)*: Jesus. *(Another one)* What are these?

PABLO: Research. I've been thinking about it for years. My fire paintings. I wake up, check the papers—anything about a fire, I'm there, digging through the ashes.

RUBY *(Another photo)*: Is this Stella Street?

PABLO: Two row homes burned to a shell. *(Another photo)* This was a house fire on Venango. *(Another one)* House fire on American Street.

RUBY: You gotta go easy on us, Pablo. You gotta go easy on yourself. *(Changing the subject)* How we gonna drag the Philly folks up?

PABLO: Good luck with that.

RUBY: Acosta and Inez would go nuts for this.

PABLO: They're kissing the mayor's ass. Acosta wants that endorsement for state senator.

RUBY: What about Rey? I bet the ride from Philly is beautiful right now.

PABLO: Doing his thing, a creature of habit.

RUBY: You finish his bike yet?

PABLO: Nah, but half the chassis has a mermaid with your mom's face.

RUBY: Are you serious?

PABLO: She was piiiiissed!

RUBY: How about Jenn? Let's go half-half on a bus ticket.

PABLO: No one's coming up from Philly, kid.

(Ruby dials on her phone.)

RUBY: An invitation never hurt.

PABLO: Don't.

RUBY: She can crash on my floor.

(He grabs her phone.)

I know things got ugly for a while but family is family.

PABLO: I never had a bone to pick with the woman.

RUBY: Has she been around at all? Still picking fights with Acosta I trust?

PABLO: He kicked her out of the squat.

RUBY: No one tells me anything.

PABLO: Your mom stopped bailing her out and Jenn took it real personal.

RUBY: Because those arrests were bullshit.

PABLO: The arrests were legit.

RUBY: For dancing?

PABLO: The woman hasn't waved a flag since . . . psh . . .

RUBY: Last summer she and I danced a frickin' marathon at the Spring Garden Bridge.

PABLO: You know she started protesting outside the bar? Shouting. With a megaphone. "Wake up! Wake up!" Your mom had to call the cops, a few times.

RUBY: Jesus Christ . . .

PABLO: Listen . . .

(Ruby does.)

Wine. I need wine.

(She grabs two glasses of wine for them.)

What time is it?

RUBY: Seriously. How long does it take to grab some fucking cheeseburgers?

PABLO: Since when do you talk like a trucker?

RUBY: Really?

(Ruby downs the wine.)

PABLO: Don't drink, okay?

RUBY: I'm practically twenty-one.

PABLO: Practically?

RUBY: I was raised in a bar.

PABLO: So next time you're in Philly ask your mom for a glass of wine.

RUBY: I don't have to ask, I'm a master of sneaking.

PABLO: Rule of thumb: have four days a week where you don't touch alcohol.

RUBY: You don't follow that rule.

PABLO: You want to be a social worker, you're gonna see some heavy stuff.

RUBY: If anyone can handle it.

PABLO: If you can't go four days without drinking you're not handling shit. Do you go four days a week without drinking?

RUBY: I'm in college. Free beer practically runs from the faucets.

PABLO: Best reason to go light on the bottle? So you never have to give up the bottle.

RUBY: I used to sneak drinks from the bar when Mom wasn't looking.

PABLO: How? She marked everything with a Sharpie. She kept an eagle's eye.

RUBY: If you take a sip from fifteen different bottles no one can tell the level's gone down.

(Daphne enters with take-out bags.)

DAPHNE: Cheeseburgers.

RUBY: I'm starving.

(They sit, begin to eat.)

DAPHNE: Milkshake? Chocolate-strawberry.

RUBY: Thanks.

(Daphne and Pablo exchange coded glances.)

DAPHNE: So listen, kiddo . . .

PABLO: Let her eat first.

RUBY: What?

(Ruby puts down her food.)

DAPHNE: We wanted to wait until the opening . . . I went back to your dorm and packed some stuff. We're heading to Philly tonight. The three of us.

RUBY: I have Econ in the morning.

DAPHNE: It's Jenn. Her . . . memorial is tomorrow.

RUBY: Memorial as in . . .

DAPHNE: I would have called on Tuesday, when it happened . . .

RUBY: As in funeral?

DAPHNE: You've been planning this for months . . .

RUBY: What are you talking about?

DAPHNE: Do you know what self-immolation means? *(Silence)* Do you know what self-immolation means?

(Daphne pulls a newspaper clipping from her purse.)

UPenn did a little write-up.

RUBY: Get that paper out of my face. Speak.

DAPHNE: Tuesday at the Love Statue. Jenn poured gasoline over her head, lit a match, and started dancing. A few people tried to douse the flames but she went very quickly.

(Silence.)

There's more details in the paper.

(Silence.)

I couldn't tell you over the phone.

(Daphne pulls a large envelope from her purse, hands it to Ruby.)

RUBY: "To Ruby Slippers from Jennifer Song."

(Ruby opens it, pulls out a thick stack of loose-leaf paper.)

"Hear ye, hear ye. Hippies and fat cats, bigwigs and small fry. Come one, come all to my final performance. Tuesday at noon at the Love Statue. Free of charge." Who did she give these to?

DAPHNE: The *Inquirer*, 1060, XPN. Friends.

RUBY: No one tried to stop her?

DAPHNE: I don't think anyone opened it in time.

RUBY: You got one, too? When did she give it to you?

DAPHNE: Tuesday. The day of.

RUBY: What time?

DAPHNE: It was at the bar door when I opened.

RUBY: You open at 10:45. This says noon. So you got it in time.

DAPHNE: Jenn was handing out leaflets and treatises all year.

RUBY: Which you ignored.

DAPHNE: You become numb to it.

RUBY *(To Pablo)*: Did you get one?

PABLO: Don't implicate me.

RUBY: Did you get a letter and when did you open it?

PABLO: Hey, my friend just committed suicide, too. Daphne's friend just committed suicide.

RUBY: This was a rallying cry. A lucid act of protest—

PABLO: Oh, bullshit.

RUBY: She was a car alarm. Noise noise noise, a fucking gnat. That's what you all thought of her.

DAPHNE: I loved her.

RUBY: You threw her clothes out the window.

DAPHNE: Because she's been planning this for years and I wanted her the hell away from you.

PABLO: How many beers did I buy the woman, huh? How many twenty-dollar bills for art supplies? It's a shitty world and Jenn couldn't deal.

(Ruby checks her phone.)

RUBY: Two missed calls, Tuesday morning, nine A.M.

(Pablo throws her phone across the room.)

PABLO: Fuck her for calling you.

RUBY: Maybe she wanted someone to stop her. I didn't call back.

PABLO: Fuck her for implicating me, or Daphne, or any of us! Fuck her for making a big production and dressing it up like some martyrdom.

RUBY: Belief, marrow-deep, so real it hurts, that was her gift. Name one thing any of us believes in? Other than the Great God Heineken?

PABLO: Life, knee-deep in the trenches, day after shitty day, that's what. Illness and stench and poverty, that's what. If you ever *think* of doing something like this, of emulating this in any way, of even *trying* to hurt yourself—

RUBY: I *should* grab the baton, if I was half the woman she was—

PABLO: I would kill you, I would kill you first!

RUBY: *You* poured the gasoline. *You* lit the match. *I* walked right on by.

PABLO: Jenn was not a hero.

RUBY: Yes she was.

PABLO: No, Ruby.

DAPHNE: She was ill. / She needed treatment.

RUBY: UNRELATED. / UNRELATED.

PABLO: Your parents threw you out with the goddamn trash, you woke up the next morning and every morning since then and decided to breathe. *That's* brave. *That's* fucking heroic. Do not let this become your Bible.

(He hurls the suicide note across the room. The pages scatter to the ground. Ruby picks up a random sheet.)

RUBY *(Reading)*:
>And so I will be your sunrise awakening
>And so I will be your torch for liberty
>And so I will try to spark the discussion
>I'll light the match of your human memory
>and come ablaze with transformation
>Wake up
>Wake up
>Wake up
>Wake up
>Wake up
>Wake up

(She finds another sheet.)

>Wake up
>Wake up
>Wake up

Wake up
Wake up

(Another sheet.)

Wake up
Wake up
Wake up.

SCENE 4

Piano music drifts in from the second-story window. We are drawn back to North Philly.

RUBY: I am twenty-five.

(Into: Daphne's Dive, five years later. The girl's sneaker has not budged from the bar. The potted aloe thrives. A Heineken poster advertises: THROWBACK NIGHT! *Wicked minor-key salsa blasts—think Ray Barretto's "Indestructible" or Eddie Palmieri's "Puerto Rico.")*

INEZ: You're not gonna dance?
DAPHNE: My stomach.
INEZ: Pues, toca el güiro!

(Daphne plays a güiro while seated.)

DAPHNE: Ruby, toca el ron!

(Ruby taps a rum bottle with a spoon.)

RUBY: Pablo, toca el bongo!

(Pablo taps a bongo.)

PABLO: Rey, toca el . . . toca el penny jar!

(Rey grabs the leave-a-penny jar, shaking it.)

ACOSTA: Should we, Mami?
INEZ: Your hernia, viejo.
ACOSTA: It's our song.

(Acosta and Inez are old-school salsa dancers—smooth and subtle. The song ends triumphantly.)

DAPHNE: Wepa!
ACOSTA: Now do that five hours straight. Man, we used to hit that dance floor!
INEZ: Ancient history.
ACOSTA: This bar is the reason we got together.
INEZ: About one Botox treatment and thirty pounds ago.
ACOSTA: Three Botoxes.
DAPHNE: I have this image of you walking through that door in hot-pink jeans and hoochie-mama stilettos.
ACOSTA: Bait and switch. She started with the orthopedic shoes the day we tied the knot.

RUBY: You guys met here?

INEZ: That was our first dance. Tell her, Papi.

ACOSTA: You never let me finish a story.

INEZ: I was very depressed. I got heavy into the spirit world, the orisha. A santero priest needed help cleaning some sacrificed chickens. So I'm alone, on a Friday night, in a ghetto kitchen defeathering chickens. Which is the dirtiest of the dirty—

REY: Oh I've defeathered a chicken or two.

INEZ: So in walks my friend . . . ¿como se llama?

ACOSTA: Gerónima.

PABLO: You did not have a friend named Gerónima.

INEZ: Oh yes.

RUBY: No actual person is named Gerónima.

ACOSTA: It's the feminine version of Jeronimoooooooo!

INEZ: So she sees me and is like, "Put the chicken down. Put that chicken down!" She took me to her house, handed me some ten-dollar-store clothes and was like, "Where to, comadre?" I was like, "My sister's new place." You had been open, what, a month?

ACOSTA: I was sitting at Rey's table. Wearing my pinstripe Armani.

INEZ: Like he was auditioning for *Goodfellas*.

ACOSTA: I had just signed the papers for the warehouse on Mascher.

INEZ: Cologne so strong my nose hair singed.

ACOSTA: Inez preferred patchouli back then.

DAPHNE: Hippie!

INEZ: Anyway, we get into a steamy fighting argument about the Equal Rights Amendment.

ACOSTA: I said come down to earth, wake up to life en el barrio.

INEZ: I said the word feminism, he stared at me with this blank look like, Huh?

DAPHNE: Yadda yadda, they get in this big fight. The room parted like the red sea. Feminists on one side, Catholics on the other. Confused people in the middle. I was like, "If one person is packing, there's gonna be a blood bath."

INEZ: So she kicked our asses out.

ACOSTA: She didn't kick us out.

INEZ: Yes, Papi.

DAPHNE: I didn't kick you out. I put on that song and was like, "Stop ruining my Friday night business."

ACOSTA: By that time we had no choice, it was like, dance or there's gonna be a riot. So. *(Clave rhythm)* Cahn-cahn, cahn-cahn-cahn. We start moving our feet and we discovered each other. I said, "You know what? This makes sense."

INEZ: And that was the key that opened the floodgate. *(Raising a shot glass)* Uno, dos, tres—

ALL: Throwback!

(They all do a shot.)

RUBY: Who's got a story about my girl Jenn?

ACOSTA: No, we're having a good time!

PABLO *(Tapping a glass)*: "Half a brain."

ACOSTA: Deep cut!

PABLO: Ruby, do you remember asking, "Where can I buy half a brain? I gotta buy half a brain!"

RUBY: You guys just make stuff up about me.

PABLO: We're all like, "Half a brain?" But you kept on about it, "Daphne wants half a brain for Christmas. I gotta buy her half a brain!"

DAPHNE: Our first holiday together.

REY: "Hey Rey, how much does half a brain cost?"

ACOSTA: "Lend me money, for half a brain."

INEZ: "Can you get half a brain at the Cherry Hill Mall?"

DAPHNE: Bendito. Christmas morning, you opened your presents: Barbies, a scooter, Nikes. Everything you wanted. You hid behind the sofa, wouldn't come out. I was like, "What happened, Ruby, you miss your mom? You miss your brothers and sisters?" You had asked what I wanted for Christmas and I had told you "peace of mind."

PABLO: A "piece" of mind equals half a brain.

DAPHNE: You were torn up not getting me what I wanted.

PABLO: Uno, dos, tres—

ALL: Throwback!

(They all do a shot. Ruby does two.)

RUBY: Jenn story! Jenn story!

PABLO: No.

INEZ: Guess what I brought . . . Throwback dessert . . .

(She presents a dessert tray.)

DAPHNE: Brownies?

INEZ: Brownies *plus.*

PABLO: Uh-oh . . .

INEZ: Hydroponic, for the stomach pain. Rey supplied, I baked.

ACOSTA: Negra! You're a senator's wife!

PABLO: State senator.

ACOSTA: I wasn't here. I didn't see nothing.

DAPHNE: I ain't eating one until you do.

PABLO: You're not that important. No one gives a shit what you eat.

REY: Don't act like you and me never shared a reefer.

DAPHNE: Yeah, back in the day? Puff puff pass.

ACOSTA: Lies, Ruby, all lies.

REY: Remember when Jenn gave Acosta psilocybin?

RUBY: Silo-whaaa?

REY: Ceremonial goodies, foraged in the wild. Not crap made out of batteries like they smoke today. Nonetheless, Acosta had a very bad trip.

ACOSTA: Shet up.

DAPHNE: Cómelo! Cómelo!

ALL: Cómelo! Cómelo!

ACOSTA: When Brownie-gate costs me the next election, and the city falls to shit, you have yourselves to blame. One, two, three—

ALL: Throwback!

(They all eat the brownies.)

INEZ *(Singsong, psychedelic)*: Wooooo-eeeee-ooooo. Groove-ay.

ACOSTA *(Confiscating Ruby's brownie)*: All right, you had your nibble.

RUBY *(Stumbling off to the bathroom)*: Whoa . . .

DAPHNE: If she makes a mess in there . . .

PABLO: High functioning is the worst kind.

DAPHNE: She's not that high functioning.

RUBY *(Returning with a tissue)*: Can I blow my nose? Relax.

(Daphne folds—a stomach pang.)

INEZ: Sis?

DAPHNE: One bite of brownie.

INEZ: Tengo papaya pills. Tengo ginger drops.

PABLO: Go to the doctor.

ACOSTA: This is every day.

DAPHNE: Let me breathe, people. *(Cutting at the aloe)* You're looking at the only thing that works. This here is my throwback. From Inez's garden to my bum stomach. Ya'll knuckleheads need to learn how nasty this tastes. All right people? Prepárense. It tastes like a monkey's ass but it's very healing. Slurp it down quick.

(She hands out little bits of aloe.)

ACOSTA: Feels like an eyeball.
REY: No smell.
INEZ: Watch, you'll be regular all week.
DAPHNE: One, two, three—
ALL: Throwback!

(They swallow the aloe—it's disgusting.)

DAPHNE: Now ya'll know!
PABLO: Rey's turn. Rey! Rey!
DAPHNE, INEZ, ACOSTA AND RUBY: Rey! Rey!
REY: I'm here as a student of life.
DAPHNE: Come on!
REY: Pass. I just want to let the brownie sink in.
RUBY: Holy Innocents graduation. When Jenn stormed the stage!
ACOSTA: Boo! I'm not singing her no swan songs!
PABLO: I'm with Acosta.
DAPHNE: Me three. Rey, you're up.
RUBY: Ya'll want a story? A real story? Jonathan, my biological brother. His hips were crooked, he couldn't walk. When I was still with my birth mom, I heard about this therapy where you bury someone up to the waist and they kick their way out. I took Jonathan to Norris Square. Pushing him in a grocery cart, burying him in the sandbox. I was ten. Other kids throwing rocks at him, yelling

"retard, faggot." But one day he kicked his way out, took a textbook step and punched me in the nose. I was smiling with a nosebleed! My first year with Mom—Daphne, Mom—every day I would beg her. "Track down Jonathan, adopt him, I'll run away if you don't, I'll kill myself if you don't." Well, after a year of that, she was so nice about it, she sat me down real gentle and was like, "Ruby I barely have the energy for you, Ruby please stop asking about Jonathan." I never said his name again. In fifteen years you heard me say it? Jonathan. Jonathan. The end!

I found him last year. Living with cousins in Jersey. I'm living like a queen, he's in a duct-taped wheelchair that looks like some garbage Pablo would paint. But did I tell you about it? Did I utter the name Jonathan?

DAPHNE: You want a trophy?

(Ruby grabs Rey's keys from the bar and exits.)

REY: Hey! Those were my keys.
PABLO: She'll end up in a ditch.
ACOSTA: Vamos. Let's go get her.
INEZ: Really James Bond? You're in no shape for a chase scene.
PABLO: I'll drive.
INEZ: You couldn't piss in a straight line.

(Pablo runs outside.)

REY: Daphne's the only one sober.
DAPHNE: I'm working. This is a work night.
ACOSTA: Close the goddamn bar and go get your daughter.
DAPHNE: Who needs a refill?
INEZ *(Looking out)*: The bike is still out there.
PABLO *(Reentering with keys)*: Look what I found.

INEZ: She's probably walking, sobering up.

DAPHNE: You mean emptying her stomach in an alley?

PABLO: I'm going to Tony's Place.

DAPHNE: Enjoy his pissy taps. City full of drunks. My lights'll stay on. Go on, all of you.

REY: The one and only time I saw Acosta cry. We were installing a glass storefront up on Allegheny. Me, Acosta, some workers. And we heard, *vrooooooooom*. Drag racing. Neon rims, holes in the muffler, the works. Meanwhile, an old man was crossing the street, one car nailed him straight on. He must've flown thirty feet through the air, and he came down hard. Seven or eight cars race by, not one of 'em stopped. The guy was losing a lot of blood. Acosta sat him on the curb, sang some Spanish songs and when that old man let out his final breath? Acosta folded like the Sunday paper, saying, "See? That's what we do to our own." We came here. I know you remember this. I know you remember, and you. Jenn said, "We're gonna throw that man a party!" Now Lord knows why, she had a bunch of bandannas. She said let's hold a vigil.

INEZ: Jenn and Pablo painted all those bandannas.

PABLO: "RIP, Anonymous."

REY: At sundown we took to the streets, waving those bandannas, Ruby with us. People coming onto their stoops, joining in, we must've marched till midnight. And who was at the very front, hand in hand, leading the way?

DAPHNE: Jenn and Acosta.

REY: One, two, three.

(He drinks.)

SCENE 5

Piano music upstairs.

RUBY: I am twenty-nine.

(Into: Daphne's Dive, four years later. The girl's sneaker holds fort on the bar. The aloe thrives. Ruby is behind the bar, cleaning glasses, wiping down the countertop. She has a few small scrapes and Band-Aids on her face and body. Rey nurses a beer, Daphne sips a ginger ale, scanning the Daily News.*)*

REY: Jenn's anniversary. Five bucks says Acosta comes.
RUBY: Bet.
REY: Bet.

(They place their bets. Pablo comes in with a cart full of salvaged junk, much of it burnt. He places a charred rice pot on the counter.)

PABLO: Is she beautiful, or is she beautiful?

RUBY: Get that shitty thing off my bar.

PABLO: There's a rotten sneaker there!

RUBY: Don't trash-talk the lucky shoe. Off.

(Pablo moves the caldero to a stool.)

Let me guess. The house fire on Waterloo?

PABLO: You should've seen me, weeping como un bebe, digging through those ashes.

RUBY: Like a kid in an egg hunt.

DAPHNE: You can take the man out the dumpster.

PABLO *(Rhapsodic)*: I was sobbing all morning. My hands are trembling.

RUBY: You actually get high from other people's suffering.

PABLO: The ashes were still warm, Ruby, the whole place down in flames, one kid in the ICU, two parakeets die, the oven crumpled como un acordeón, and what survives it all?

DAPHNE: The caldero.

PABLO: The rice pot the family brought from the island.

RUBY: That family lost everything. Don't steal the damn pot, it's all they have.

PABLO: You know how many mouths it has fed? On the news it said nine children lived there.

RUBY: Stop having babies, people.

REY: I'm one of eight.

PABLO: Youngest of twenty-three.

DAPHNE: I thought it was twenty.

PABLO: Mami was pregnant from puberty to death. When I was born she had arthritis. One day she was in the backyard hanging clothes to dry. She felt another one coming, called out to my pop. He found a branch on the avocado tree, lifted her up, hoisted both arms over the branch, positioned himself below her, hands out. She didn't have to push. She was so loose it was just pfft—gravity. And thus I entered this world.

(There is a gift in his shopping cart wrapped in newspaper. He presents it to Daphne.)

DAPHNE: Don't give me no junk from that fire.

PABLO: It's from Sears.

DAPHNE: It's not my birthday.

PABLO: Can't a man give you a box?

(Daphne unwraps it: a coffeemaker.)

DAPHNE: Fool. My Krups broke twenty years ago!

PABLO: I know, I've been sleepy ever since.

RUBY: Someone's being awful nice . . .

DAPHNE: Not my trash.

PABLO: Daphne . . .

RUBY: They're my dumpsters now. Have at 'em.

PABLO: Don't joke, you two. *(Suddenly on one knee)* Will you marry me?

REY: Oh shit.

DAPHNE: You're proposing with a coffeemaker? Am I not worth a microwave? Can I get a dishwasher up in here?

PABLO: Óyeme, Daphne, en serio. So you're a lesbian, so what? We'll make an arrangement.

DAPHNE: I'm not a lesbian.

PABLO: You're something.

DAPHNE: A woman who does not need to be cooking no man three hot meals a day.

PABLO: I'll take one hot meal. My joints creak to sit down or stand up. Every day I spend an hour plucking out grays.

RUBY: Cuz he's a vain son-of-a-bitch.

PABLO: Two more blinks of the eye, I'll be on my deathbed and with who at my side? I don't want to leave this world alone, Daphne. Do you?

(Pablo stands there, serious as stone. Daphne scrutinizes his eyes, their noses almost touching.)

DAPHNE: Motherfucker . . .

PABLO: But you were considering! Eh? Eh?

DAPHNE *(Slapping him)*: Asshole!

PABLO: She almost said yes!

RUBY: You're sick in the head.

PABLO: It's for Jenn's anniversary. Coffee and rum, that was her drink. So brew me a Bustelo, woman!

DAPHNE: I ain't brewing you shit.

REY: Two coffees, Ruby!

DAPHNE: Make that three. So I can throw one in his face!

RUBY: You would think, with that fancy museum on the horizon, you could fake propose with a real cubic zirconia.

DAPHNE: At the very least.

PABLO: The Ernst Museum! Oye, my art's flying first class, but I fly economy.

(Acosta enters.)

REY: El jefe!

ACOSTA: Block looks good!

PABLO: Long time no see!

RUBY: Didn't think you'd be through.

REY: I had faith. *(Takes the bet money from the bar)*

ACOSTA: What are you doing back there?

RUBY: New sign's going up soon. Pablo did the letters in gold leaf. Ruby's Daphne's Dive.

DAPHNE: I got my house in P.R. I'm going back to my old country shack! Three rooms built into the mountain. Two stilts on one side. A back porch facing the flamboyán trees. A babbling brook. A hammock.

RUBY: But no alarm clock upstairs. No more waking up to Mozart.

DAPHNE: My stomach is my alarm clock. Goes off all night. Come July, I wave good-bye.

ACOSTA: So find someone to run the place. I got plenty of good workers.

RUBY *(Referring to the soda gun)*: This little device right here? I press a thing, tonic water comes out. Outside those doors? Chaos, insanity. In here, soda at the press of a button.

ACOSTA: You two are always pulling shit like this without telling me. I'm the godfather, ask my advice.

RUBY: How? A courier pigeon? Stop by, you want the scoop.

ACOSTA: Is Inez coming today?

RUBY: She better.

ACOSTA: Is it okay that I'm here?

RUBY: Ask her, not me.

ACOSTA: Did she tell you?

RUBY: I read the paper.

(Ruby swallows a few pills.)

ACOSTA: You have to do that in front of me?

RUBY: Xanax would do you a world of good. How's the rec center?

ACOSTA: Has Inez mentioned anything?

RUBY: About chicky girl? Barbara? Barbie?

DAPHNE: Ruby.

RUBY: How's the rec center?

ACOSTA: The ribbon cutting is Sunday.

PABLO: That thing sparkles like a diamond.

REY: I etched my name into one of the windows. "Rey was here!"

ACOSTA: Did you tell them your next job?

REY: I don't want to make Pablo jealous.

PABLO: Of you?

ACOSTA: Rey's picking up a paintbrush.

REY: Yup, painting yellow lines on every street in the city. No one stops to think, where do those lines come from?

ACOSTA: I got a manager position with your name on it.

PABLO: Nah.

RUBY: Pablo's at the museum level now. He's on that European tip.

(Inez enters.)

INEZ: Hello beautiful people.

DAPHNE: Hey gorgeous. Takes one to know one.

RUBY: Ready to get this party started?

INEZ *(Noticing Ruby's cuts)*: What the hell? What happened to your face?

RUBY *(Referring to Acosta)*: Thank you. Some people didn't notice. I took a ride on the Mermaid Express.

INEZ *(To Rey)*: You let her on your bike?

RUBY: I got home, pulled off my helmet, fell over parking the damn thing. You two gonna say hello to each other?

INEZ: Hi.

ACOSTA: Hi.

RUBY: I've been thinking. Joint custody. Acosta gets the bar Monday through Thursday. Inez gets it on weekends. You alternate Fridays. Cool?

ACOSTA: Did you get my message, negra?

INEZ: Not negra. Call me Inez, por favor?

ACOSTA: Inez.

INEZ: Yes, I got your message.

ACOSTA: What do you say? Dinner? Indian Palace, tonight?

INEZ: Ruby, I was clearing out the yard, getting ready for the move. I don't mind selling the furniture, the tchotchkes, not even the house. Woman to woman? Enjoy everything, require nothing. I used to walk the city barefoot. It's not that I didn't have the hottest shoes in Philly, it was a statement. I had my feet. And I still got 'em. But the garden? Saying good-bye to those güiro vines? *(Digs a green sprout from her purse)* It's the original root from the aloe plant. A voice told me, put it in your bag, it'll find the right home. For all those cuts. You look like the day we found you.

RUBY *(Tenderly)*: Let the man buy you one plate of Indian food.

INEZ: Not today, sweetie. *(Then, with a burst of energy, clapping for attention)* Listen people, parking's gonna be a nightmare! I drove by the Love Statue. Occupy Philly's taken over half of Market Street! Green-haired punks, Tibetan lamas, nuns, Angela Davis—*the* Angela Davis, looking fabulous, on a milk crate with a bullhorn! Jenn belongs right there with them.

RUBY: Jenn should've held out. Occupy would've been her moment. I dug up one of her old banners. "In case of financial collapse, party in the streets!"†

—————
†A Kathy Chang(e) original quote.

INEZ: I got a carful of flowers. I bought out the florist.

REY: I got candles.

PABLO: I'll brew rum and coffee later.

DAPHNE: I found an old love letter. Take it for me? My damn stomach . . .

ACOSTA: I'll pay my respects here. I have a thing at City Hall.

RUBY: What thing?

ACOSTA: It's an election cycle.

RUBY: Are you serious? You're that busy?

ACOSTA: Ruby, I have a job to do.

RUBY: So do I. You're coming to the Love Statue. New house rules. And don't be trying to sneak away after ten minutes. Especially if news cameras show up.

(He doesn't respond. Ruby finds a printout on the wall— one of many frames collected over the years, randomly placed in the collage of life.)

I used to touch this thing and lightning would shoot through my fingers.

(Ruby chugs down a stiff gulp of rum.)

ACOSTA: Ruby.

RUBY *(Pouring rum on the ground)*: Pour one out for my sister.

(She passes it to Rey, who pours some on the ground.)

REY: Mourn you till I join you.

RUBY *(Reading)*:
> O steadfast commoners
> glowing in your everydayness
> alive as grass and sky,

the seed of transformation is in your palm.
O common folk, O beautiful ordinary
you can be revolution
you need only plant the seed.

(Jenn appears.)

JENN AND RUBY:

For years I have danced a joyous refrain
and been mocked, a cosmic fool
for the crime of insisting:

JENN:

You are revolution.
But you need a louder alarm clock
to shake the cobwebs from your eyes
Armageddon isn't D-days or mushroom clouds
it's the moment the tree forgets the soil
And so I will be your sunrise awakening
And so I will be your torch for liberty
And so I will try to spark the discussion
I'll light the match of your human memory
and come ablaze with transformation
Wake up
Wake up
Wake up
Wake up
Wake up

(Inez taps Ruby's shoulder, coaxing her out of her reverie.)

INEZ: Lista, Ruby? The Love Statue is waiting.
REY: Ruby Slippers, vamoose!

PABLO: Hello? Anybody home?
ACOSTA: You all right, kid?

(Jenn's gone.)

RUBY: Sure.
REY: Sure as eggs is eggs?
PABLO: Sure as shit?
RUBY: Let's go party in the street.
INEZ *(To Daphne)*: Join us!
DAPHNE: Someone's gotta hold down the fort.
INEZ: Wepa! Peace! Liberty! Ecology! Democracy!

(They all file out. Ruby pauses at the threshold, calling after them:)

RUBY: I'll be right out! Pull the car around!

(Ruby stands at the door.)

I am eleven.

(The bar has crawled back into the past. The girl's sneaker is gone. Ruby is younger, the cuts on her face now a healed version of her original fallen self. Daphne is younger, too, like when we first met her. A duffel is slung over Ruby's shoulder. She stands at the door, looking out.)

DAPHNE: Standing there isn't going to make the clock tick any faster.
RUBY: She ain't coming.
DAPHNE: There was probably a holdup at the courthouse. Be patient. Ruby, sit down, the chair won't bite you.

RUBY: Ow. My fucking shoulder.

DAPHNE: I put the tiger balm in your bag. Make sure she puts fresh Band-Aids on you. There's two things of Neosporin.

RUBY: I can put on my own Band-Aids.

DAPHNE: Change them daily or they'll get infected. You got your new outfits, your new sneakers. Your notebooks.

RUBY: Why you acting all peaches and cream?

DAPHNE: Call me, okay? Just cuz your mom made bail doesn't mean we can't be friends.

RUBY: I bet when you got cut your mom put Neosporin all over that shit.

DAPHNE: Enough with the hood talk.

RUBY: I bet she did.

DAPHNE: Mami was servicial. Always serving the men first, pouring orange soda for the kids.

RUBY: Same like you.

DAPHNE: No, that's my nightmare. There's a line where being humble isn't cool. Her back was so hunched from waiting on my father, her eyelashes grazed the damn ground.

RUBY: He bossed her around?

DAPHNE: She stood up for herself *one* time. Back in P.R. there was a contest: who on the island could make the best caldo santo? Holy broth. A seafood soup with coconut milk. Now, everyone in Naguabo knew: Mami made an ass-banging caldo santo. But Papi wouldn't let her go. He thought she would run off with a man. Because we were on the east coast and the competition was on the south coast, in Santa Isabel. People would walk for miles from all corners of the island to line up. Everyone carrying their lucky pot. People were so poor they'd put the soup in old buckets. Everyone wanted that blue ribbon. So Mami ignored Pop, cooked that soup for days, our casita smelled like heaven, but when time came to go,

Papi stood blocking the door. He said, "You'll have to kill me first."

RUBY: Whaaaa?

DAPHNE: Inez and I were crying. "Let her go, Papi!" People could hear from the street. The neighbors started coming up the porch, shouting through the windows. "You better let her go!" Because they had all seen his abuse and held their tongue for too long. The mayor of Naguabo showed up, said he would have Pop arrested! La policia were out front, Ruby! Papi was cornered so he said, "Give me your shoe."

RUBY: Okay . . .

DAPHNE: And Mami did and as she walked out that door he said, "You won't make it very far with only one shoe!" Mami came home five days later, her left foot bloody, blistered, raw—with a blue ribbon pinned to her dress.

RUBY: Damn. Just buy another shoe.

DAPHNE: There wasn't Payless back then. There wasn't Kmart en el campo.

RUBY: Couldn't someone give her a flip-flop?

DAPHNE: Remember, Mami was servicial. Suffering was her thing. She took more pride in that bloody foot than in the blue ribbon.

(Ruby takes off her shoe and puts it on the bar.)

RUBY: I won't make it very far with one shoe.

DAPHNE: Sweetheart. Your mom'll be here any second, put it back on. It doesn't belong here. It's not mine to keep.

(Ruby doesn't.)

RUBY: Why'd you tell me that story, then?

DAPHNE: I don't know. It's a terrible story, it's a completely messed-up story. I had a real nice week with you. You're a phenomenal girl.

RUBY: Don't insult me.

DAPHNE: I mean it.

RUBY: Then why can't I stay?

DAPHNE: Because you make me raw, like Mami's bloody foot. Don't freak out, okay?

(Daphne takes Ruby's hand, guides it under her shirt onto her belly.)

RUBY: What is that?

DAPHNE: My scar. I had a C-section.

RUBY: Damn, that's one bumpy scar. Does it hurt?

DAPHNE: I didn't care for it properly. It got infected. It messed me up inside, too. I was twelve years old.

RUBY: You got knocked up at twelve? Who was the dad?

(Daphne pulls away.)

There's stuff I want to forget, too. Please?

(A horn honks outside.)

DAPHNE: It's her.

RUBY: Can I stay one more night?

DAPHNE: Jesus Christ! Fine.

RUBY: What are you gonna tell her?

DAPHNE: Your shoe got messed up . . . You're buying new ones. At King of Prussia which is a long way so you'll be home late. I'll bring you to her first thing in the morning.

RUBY: If you're here, who'd I go shopping with?

DAPHNE: I don't know, Jenn.

RUBY: Inez and Acosta. Less suspicious. What happened to my shoe?

(Daphne nails the shoe on the bar counter.)

DAPHNE: You stepped on a nail. Evidence, I have to go show her something! Shit. It's stuck.

(Upstairs, the pianist sits and plays. The sound bleeds through the walls and open windows: the piano song, the car honking.)

END OF PLAY